THE ULTIMATE GUIDE TO MINECRAFT CREATIVE MODE

Published in 2022 by Welbeck Editions
An Imprint of Welbeck Children's Limited,
part of the Welbeck Publishing Group
Offices in: London - 20 Mortimer Street, London W1T 3JW
& Sydney - 205 Commonwealth Street, Surry Hills 2010
www.welbeckpublishing.com

Author: Eddie Robson
Designed and packaged by: Dynamo Limited
Design Manager: Sam James
Editorial Manager: Joff Brown
Production: Melanie Robertson

ISBN: 978 1 83935 218 8
Printed in Heshan, China

10 9 8 7 6 5 4 3 2 1

All game information correct as of October 2022

INDEPENDENT AND UNOFFICIAL

THE ULTIMATE GUIDE TO MINECRAFT CREATIVE MODE

MAKE YOUR OWN AMAZING MINECRAFT BUILDS!

MORTIMER

CONTENTS

WELCOME TO MINECRAFT CREATIVE

Creative offers you an infinite box of bricks—and you don't even have to clean up afterward!

EXCITEMENT IS BUILDING—LITERALLY!

While some players love *Minecraft* for its exploration, adventure, and the satisfaction of making a home out of materials they've harvested and crafted all by themelves, others are in it to express their creativity. In this book we'll show you techniques to take your builds to the next level and even develop them into your own minigames for your friends to play.

NO HEALTH OR HUNGER

It can be hard to focus on an epic build when you're constantly stopping to eat or being attacked by skeletons. In Creative you don't have to worry about any of that. (In the game world, that is—Remember to stop and eat in real life!)

ABILITY TO FLY

In Survival you have to stand on your build as you make it, which can be limiting—and annoying when you fall off and die. Being able to hover in the air gives you more freedom and lets you to see your build from all angles.

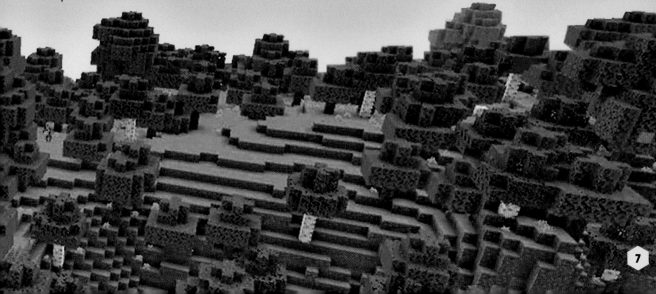

BUILDING BASICS

Creative mode offers a whole world of possibilities—but there are techniques and approaches that you'll use again and again.

Sometimes times a little planning goes a long way. Read on to find out all the best beginner's knowledge and techniques . . .

BLOCK CHOICE

In Creative you're not limited by what blocks you can mine—but having too much choice can be a problem!

CREATIVE SPECIALS

Mob eggs, enemy spawners, and command blocks can't be found in Survival, but they are in Creative. These features give you more control over your world, and mean Creative isn't just about building your own structures and then admiring them (although it can be, of course). You can make the environment come alive, and even create your own mini-game experiences.

LOOKS VS. FUNCTION

Depending on how you plan to use your builds, you may need to think more about how they look, or how they behave. If you're just into building for its own sake, don't worry too much about what a material is, just find the block that looks right. But if stuff is actually going to be happening in your world, consider things like toughness and flammability.

MIX IT UP

The mix of materials is vital. If you only use one or two types of block, your build will probably look a bit boring. If you use too many different types, your build might end up looking chaotic.

So experiment with different types of block before you start. Try laying a bunch of them on the ground as a kind of color palette to see how well they work together.

VINTAGE STYLE

If you want a building to look old, mix in some cracked and mossy stones—or even a few stones of a different type. If you want it to look like it's been repaired, use mismatched materials. For a more modern look, concrete and polished stone are best.

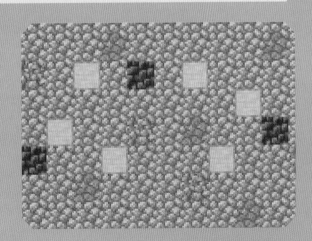

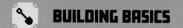

SYMMETRY

From the first block you place, choosing symmetry or asymmetry will affect your build.

WHAT IS SYMMETRY?

Symmetry just means each side of something is a mirror image of the other. It's helpful in planning out a build because you just have to repeat on one side what you've already done on the other. A symmetrical building will have an orderly look, and if you want a classical style—like something from Ancient Greece or Rome, a palace or a stately home, or just a tidy-looking house—orderly is probably the way to go.

WHY USE ASYMMETRY?

If you think about buildings in real life, many of them aren't symmetrical. A lot of houses will have the door on one side, for instance, which is a more modern approach to building. You can make a build look more interesting by making it asymmetric—and if you want it to look organic, like the tree house we'll show you later in the book, you'll definitely want to use asymmetry.

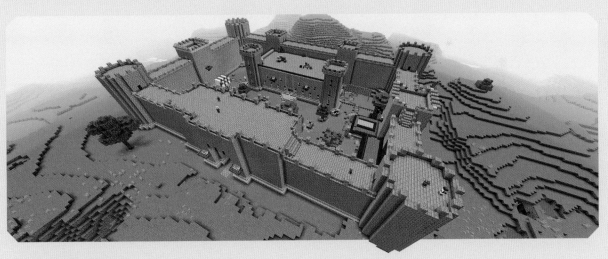

A BIT OF BOTH

You can even combine symmetry and asymmetry in the same build. Say you have a courtyard with buildings around the edges: you could make the buildings themselves asymmetrical, but use a symmetrical layout for the whole courtyard. Then the buildings on one side will mirror those on the other side.

CURVES

Minecraft blocks are kind of . . . blocky.
But there are ways around that!

GOING IN CIRCLES

To keep things simple, everything in *Minecraft* is made up of right angles. But there are ways of putting these angles together to create something like a curve. Blocks don't have to be used in the way they were intended! For example, use steps and tiles at different angles to create different edges from the standard block. You can also copy the shapes below to create easy circles in *Minecraft*.

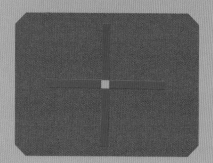 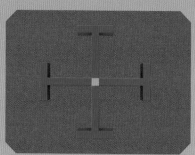 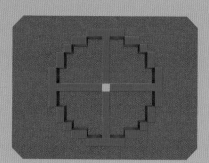

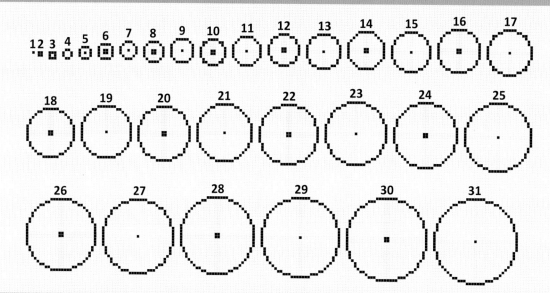

MAKE A SPHERE

Here's a handy guide to creating a sphere that's 16 blocks high. Start with level 1, build level 2 on top of that, and keep going until you reach levels 8 and 9. Then go back down the levels. You can adapt this for domes by skipping some or all of levels 1-8.

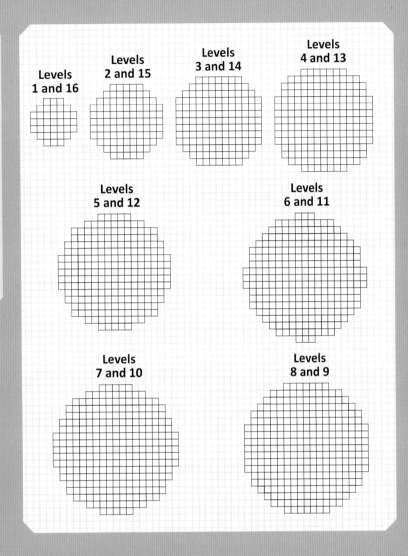

Levels 1 and 16

Levels 2 and 15

Levels 3 and 14

Levels 4 and 13

Levels 5 and 12

Levels 6 and 11

Levels 7 and 10

Levels 8 and 9

CURVES VS. ANGLES

Both of these are valid design choices—the angle has a neater look; the curve looks more like part of the natural landscape.

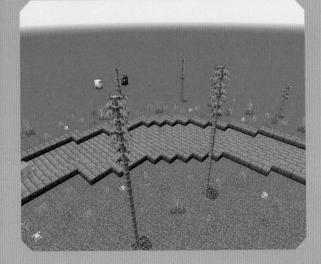

BIOMES

Minecraft offers different environments for different experiences.

WHAT'S A BIOME?

In geography, a "biome" means the particular combination of plants and animals that live in an environment such as a forest or desert. In *Minecraft,* we use it to mean a region of the game's world. Finding the right biome for your build makes sense—if you want to build a pyramid, find some desert.

WEATHER CYCLES

While you're building, you may want to set the weather to be fine and for it to be always daytime. Some themed builds may look best in darkness or rain.

MOBS ON OR OFF

"Mob" is short for "mobile object"—all other creatures in the world are mobs. Turning mob spawning off is a handy alternative to Peaceful Mode as it lets you choose to spawn mobs via eggs.

BIOME TYPES

There are seven main categories of biome: **Snowy, Cold, Temperate, Warm, Aquatic, Cave,** and **Neutral.** (The Nether and the End have their own biomes.) Within each category of biome, there are several sub-categories. Some will generate at particular heights or in particular situations, like where the land meets the sea.

DEFAULT WORLD

The default settings will randomly generate a world with a mix of biomes and with different heights of land. You can choose to just work with this, and explore it to find the type of land you want for your build.

FLAT/SUPERFLAT WORLD

You can choose to have a fairly flat landscape, so you won't have to demolish a mountain to expand your town. You can even have a totally featureless world—useful for testing things out, but most builds look better in a more interesting landscape!

CUSTOM WORLD

With custom settings, you can set it so certain biomes won't occur in your world, as well as setting things like the depth of the bedrock (the level you can't dig through). Java Edition offers even more custom options, if that's what you're into.

COMMANDS

Commands can save you a huge amount of time when working on larger projects.

COMMANDS

Any large build in *Minecraft* involves a fair bit of repetitive work, filling in walls and floors. That's why commands were introduced, to make things easier. They involve typing into the chat bar (press T to open it), and can be used to easily generate flat surfaces, replace certain blocks, and create or delete large numbers of blocks. No more destroying every block in a wall so you can move it two spaces back!

FILL IT IN!

The fill command can be used to create larger shapes and flesh out your builds. It saves you from having to lay every block individually and can take seconds, instead of hours.

COORDINATES

To use the fill command, it is important to understand coordinates. You can view your coordinates by selecting the option "display coordinates" in the game settings.

The length of the three axes is equal to the size of one block.

The **X axis** measures the longitude (east or west).
The **Y axis** measures the elevation (how high or low).
The **Z axis** measures the latitude (north or south).

CUBE COORDINATING

When looking at your coordinates, you will see three numbers. These relate to your position on the axis. The first number is your X value, the second is your Y value, and the third is your Z value.

The fill command requires you to tell the game two points you want to fill between, as well as what material you want to fill the space with.

To build a cube, stand the first corner of the cube where you want it to be and note down your coordinates. Then travel to the furthest opposite corner of where you want the cube to be and do the same. Once you have these two sets of coordinates, you can fill the space between them by writing out a fill command, like below.

/fill 0 0 0 10 10 10 concrete 0

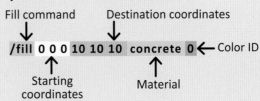

This tells the game to fill from the X, Y, Z coordinates of 0, 0, 0 to the X, Y, Z coordinates of 10, 10, 10 with white concrete. Concrete is the block's ID, and the 0 refers to the block's color ID. This number can be changed to give a different color result. There are many resources online that list all of the block IDs and color values.

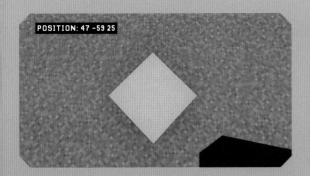

POSITION: 47 -59 25

POSITION: 57 -50 35

CUBECRAFT

Here you can see our coordinates while on top of the yellow block (our cube's first corner), and our coordinates while standing over the purple block (the opposite corner). Now all we need to do is enter the following command:

/fill 47 -59 25 57 -50 35 concrete 0

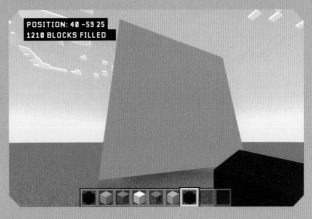

POSITION: 40 -59 25
1210 BLOCKS FILLED

ALL ABOUT THE TILDE

Once you understand how coordinates work, you can try an even quicker way of using the fill command—the tilde symbol. When writing coordinates in your command bar, you can use the tilde symbol (~) to refer to your own position, without having to know your exact coordinates. For example, ~~~ would refer to your exact position at all three coordinate points.

Adding a number after the tilde symbol would refer to a position that is that many blocks away from you. So ~10~10~10 would be 10 blocks away from you on all axes. ~10~~ would be 10 blocks away from your position on the X axis only, ~~10~ would be 10 blocks along the Y axis, and ~~~10 would be 10 blocks along the Z axis.

CUBE EXTENSION

Here we demonstrate how to build a cuboid, showing how the axis corresponds to the shape we're building. The yellow block is the starting position. The red, green, and blue blocks show how many blocks to count for the final command.

Enter: **/fill ~~~ ~4~2~6 concrete 0**

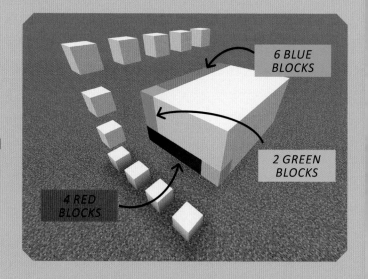

6 BLUE BLOCKS

2 GREEN BLOCKS

4 RED BLOCKS

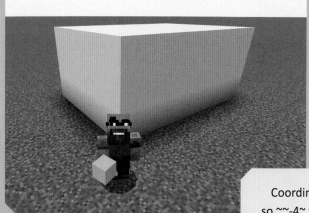

This will tell the game to build from your position to **4 blocks on the X axis, 2 blocks up on the Y axis and 6 blocks on the Z axis**. It results in a cuboid with dimensions of 5 x 3 x 7, because your starting position is 1 x 1 x 1, and you're telling it how many blocks to add.

Coordinates can also run into negative values, so ~~-4~ would build 4 blocks down on the Z axis.

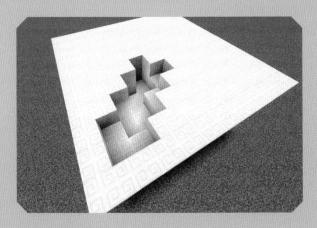

SOLID SHAPE

Solid shapes might seem a bit dull, but they can be particularly useful if you want to start carving a more complex shape, like a sculptor carving away at a boulder.

EMPTY SPACE

If you would rather make a hollow shape, you can modify the command with the word "hollow." This will build a one-block-thick hollow shape to your stated coordinates. It's really useful for building rooms and other living spaces.

For example, why not try this:
/fill ~~~ ~5~10~5 quartz_block 1 hollow

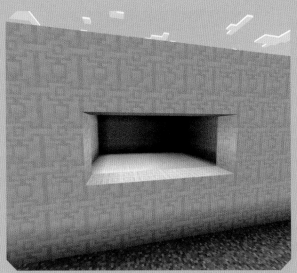

MAKE A SPLASH
Use the command:

/fill ~~~ ~8~3~8 water

Try removing the top of a hollow shape and filling it with water. We did this here by using the purple block as a starting point and counting how many blocks away from it we wanted to fill.

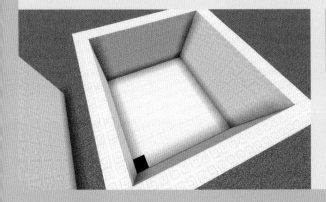

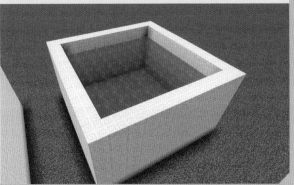

FINER DETAILS

Here we have replaced some blocks with prismarine to add texture to our build, but what if you want to swap the original quartz with something else? Well, the game has a "replace" command that allows you to replace any block, within your given coordinates, with any other block. We've marked our desired range with a purple block and a yellow block. We are going

to replace the quartz blocks with white concrete, using the command modifier "replace." Type out the fill command as normal, adding your desired material after the coordinates. Then use "replace" and type the ID of the block you are replacing.

Like this: **/fill ~~~ ~11~6~11 concrete 0 replace quartz_block 1**

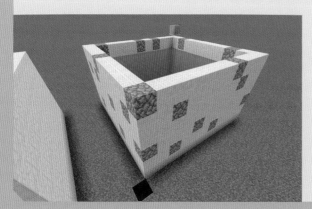
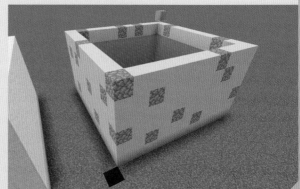

COPY AND PASTE

One of the most useful commands in *Minecraft* is the "clone" command. This can help you copy builds to another location instantly. Cloning requires three sets of coordinates. The first

two sets of X, Y, Z are the target range, and the third set is the specific block we want the build to be copied to. We did this with:

/clone -4 60 61 8 -53 73 -4 -60 81

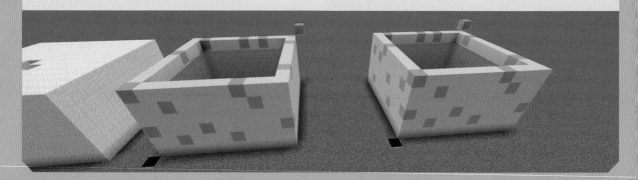

CHANGE IT UP

Here we show how you could clone and then quickly replace materials on your build.

Use: **/fill ~~~ ~11~6~11 wood 1 replace concrete 0**

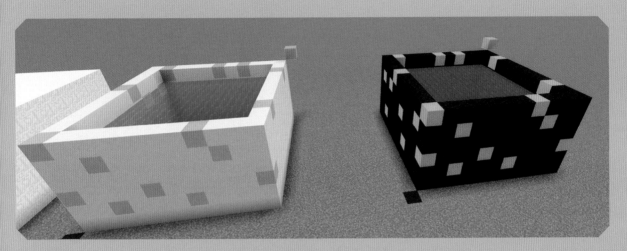

NOW IT'S YOUR TURN!

Here is an example of how you could use these principles to copy an entire build and then quickly replace blocks to add variation. Using these techniques can make building something like a village much quicker, and it greatly simplifies putting together your bigger builds. Which leaves you more time to get creative!

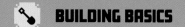

TEXTURES

Using different surfaces and effects can really bring your build to life.

PERFECT PATTERNS

The texture of a block is the pattern on its surfaces—the vast majority of *Minecraft* blocks use a pattern divided along a 16x16 grid. Downloadable texture packs are available to change the appearance of blocks and items, which may help you get the look you want. If you have the Java Edition you can also use shaders, a type of mod which alters things like shadows on objects and reflections on water.

GLASS

Usually, glass in *Minecraft* is transparent—but with the right shaders, you can make it more reflective, as you can see here. This can really transform a space by reflecting light, but you may need a powerful computer to run it!

IDEAL HOMES

Many *Minecraft* players' first Creative build is a house—and why not? We all like to imagine living in our ideal home, and *Minecraft* gives you everything you need to create it. If you want to make a really personal build, a house is a perfect project!

HOME

If you could live anywhere, where would you live?

A DESIGN FOR LIFE

If you've played Survival, you'll probably have already built a house, even if it's just a small wooden shack to stay safe in. But in Creative you can be much more ambitious!

BUILT BY: **NICKHMC**

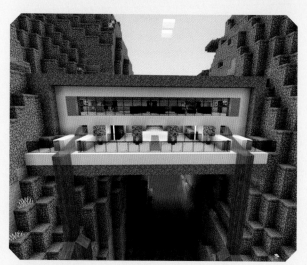

HOLIDAY VILLA

This villa on a private island blends nicely into the landscape—the trees give it a private, secluded feel. It's also a good example of asymmetric building—the columns around the veranda at the front are a great touch.

CANYON HOUSE

Homes that might be a tad impractical in reality can be easily achieved in *Minecraft*, as this house straddling a canyon shows. The smooth white modernist design contrasts nicely with the moss blocks that blend it with the landscape.

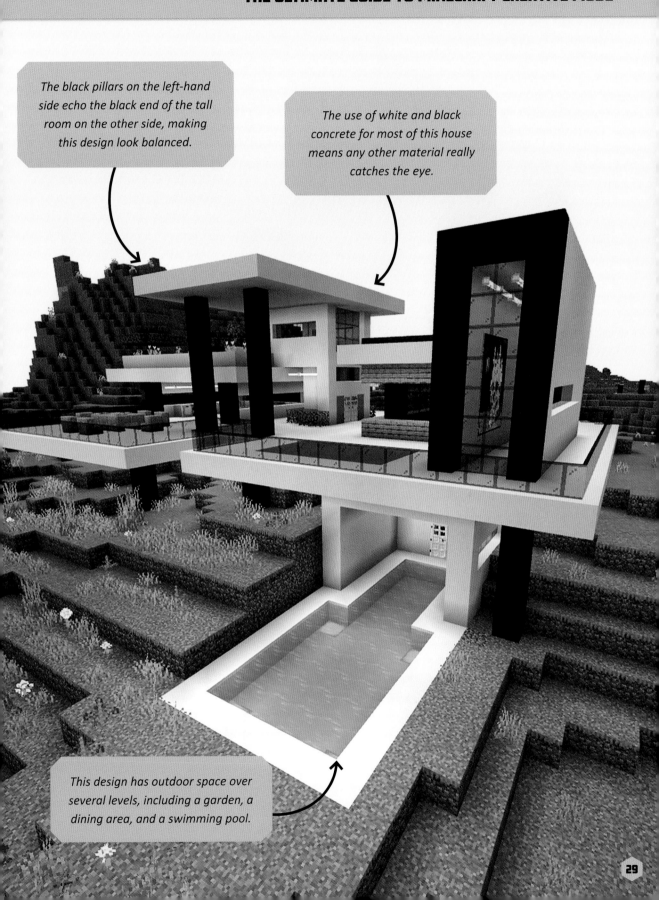

The black pillars on the left-hand side echo the black end of the tall room on the other side, making this design look balanced.

The use of white and black concrete for most of this house means any other material really catches the eye.

This design has outdoor space over several levels, including a garden, a dining area, and a swimming pool.

SAVANNAH HOUSE

This build uses the brighter colors offered by acacia planks. The fence posts used around the windows are a great example of using something differently from how it was intended—they're much slimmer than normal blocks.

TUDOR HOUSE

The Tudor style used large beams of solid wood for the frame of the house, and that is cleverly reflected in this design—this builder has made the beams from dark oak logs, rather than planks. Planks are used for the detail around the beams.

MANSION

A grand house needs a grand setting—the garden of a house like this is just as important as the building itself. The symmetry of this garden makes it look very designed and crafted, and reflects the symmetry of the house.

ECO HOUSE

This is designed to blend in with the landscape, so the main material is wooden planks. A layer of soil on the roof supports a pond, meaning the house is hardly visible from above!

MODERN HOUSE

The modern style uses light-colored materials (quartz, in this case) and has flat roofs and floor-to-ceiling windows. With such a simple design, the choice of secondary material is important: the bare brick contrasts nicely with the smoothness of the main material.

BUILT BY: **TOMONMARS**

TIDY COTTAGE

There's lots of symmetry in this design—even the hedges under the windows, and the flowerpots. The shutters are spruce trapdoors. They won't close over the windows, but they look the part!

ACACIA TERRACE

The patterns on the surfaces of certain blocks can be used as a design element—for instance, the "rings" in acacia logs look more like a geometric paving design when set into the ground, as in this build.

RETURN TO ENDER

You'll probably recognize this as an End Portal frame block, but here it's been used as a fence-mounted mailbox—the shapes on each side really do look like slots. Just hope your mail doesn't get sent to the End . . .

FOUNDATION COURSE

The deep slate base of this house is a nice detail, setting it apart from the landscape. Mangrove slabs have been used to create a roof with a shallower pitch than one made out of steps, and the color is echoed in the lantern holder.

BUILT BY: **SOPHIE**

BUILT BY: **GABRIEL ROBSON SPOONER**

HARBOR HOUSE

This safe haven from sea storms is a good example of using three main materials—oak, quartz and warped wood—to give a build variety while not making it too busy. The fence posts underneath fill that side while still letting in light.

AN EARTHY LOOK

This house is built into a hillside, so mud bricks and compacted mud blocks have been used to give it a look that matches with the surrounding environment. Trapdoors have been used to make the front door taller.

FOCAL POINTS

People tend to arrange their living room furniture to face something—like this fireplace with a picture above it. Note the use of trapdoors to enhance the chairs—trapdoors have many different uses in interior design!

FEELING SHELF-ISH

Whole walls of bookshelves take up a lot of space and can be boring to look at, so break it up a little—this design incorporates a lectern, which goes nicely with the shelves, as well as a chest and a lantern.

ALCOVES

Shelves and storage spaces are often set into the walls of houses, so remember your walls don't have to be completely flat. This one incorporates two bookshelves—just keep in mind what this will look like from the other side.

CUT A RUG

Use wool to give your interiors a softer feel. You can create carpets by simply placing two wool blocks next to each other on the second row of the crafting grid.

ENTERTAINMENT SYSTEMS

The simplest way of creating a TV in *Minecraft* is to make it wall-mounted. The record player next to it is simply an item frame with a music disc in it—shame you can't place one of these on a jukebox!

PURPLE PATCH

It's nice to echo colors in different areas of a room. Here, the chairs and table (made of purple with crimson sides) match the lamp (a pearlescent froglight) and the purple candle at the far end.

MODERN KITCHEN

There's so much creative use of different objects here! The oven is made from glowing item frames with trapdoors for stovetops. The cabinets use acacia trapdoors. Saplings in pots make good plants. A brewing stand and food items on the worktops complete the scene.

CHECKER IT OUT

A black-and-white checkered floor looks stylish in a kitchen—this one uses quartz pillars for extra texture. Shelves are created by adding trapdoors, a grindstone makes a knife holder, and the shelves of cookbooks are a neat addition.

OUTDOOR KITCHEN

This beach bar and kitchen uses a row of brewing stands to represent a shelf of bottles above the serving area. The subtle pattern of the back counter is created by using shulker boxes— which can also be used for storage.

BUILT BY: **EVERYTHINGBURRITO1**

TILED BATHROOM

The clean, minimal design of modern bathrooms is well suited to *Minecraft*. Here, the tiles only go halfway up the wall, which contrasts with the smoothly-blended white concrete. A grindstone has been repurposed as a shower head!

STONE BATHROOM

The calcite walls here create a classy effect. The towel hanging on the wall is a plain banner, and the unlit candles at the edge of the bath look like bottles of shampoo.

BUILT BY: **GABRIEL ROBSON SPOONER**

ORNAMENTS

Fine details can be tricky in *Minecraft*, but they make a place feel more like a home: using this mob skull as a decoration is a good idea because these items always face you as you place them, so you can place them at a diagonal angle. This gives the room a more casual real-life feel.

MAXIMIZING SPACE

This design creates a raised cabin-style bed by placing a normal bed on top of two trapdoors, leaving space underneath for a crafting table and bookshelf. Just make sure you've got somewhere to put a ladder!

MUSHROOM BEDROOM

A simple design theme can be echoed in different areas of a room—this one builds the bed from mushroom blocks instead of using a regular bed, and repeats that on the floor to make a rug. Mushrooms on the bedside tables complete the design.

FOUR-POSTER BED

Now this is really fancy! An old-fashioned style of bed is simple to create with fences. A real one would have had curtains that could be drawn aside. You could recreate that by adding more banners to the frame.

CABIN BED

A bed doesn't just have to stand on its own—here it's part of a multi-functional piece of furniture with shelves and a barrel "cabinet" on one side, and a ladder leading to the bed on the other. Scaffolding with a trapdoor attached makes a chair.

FANCY BEDROOM

Another enhanced bed here, with blocks of wood used to make a more substantial headboard and trapdoors at the end. Additional trapdoors create shelves at the side and above, and again we've got a matching rug to tie the room together.

UNDERGROUND BASE

Join the underground movement!

ALL ABOUT THAT BASE

Few things in life are as satisfying as an underground base—and in *Minecraft* you can make them as broad and deep as you want without the usual worries about sinkholes. And since there's no exterior, you can focus completely on the interior!

FRAME IT

You can just carry your tools or keep them in a chest—but putting them in item frames adds to the overall sense of what a room is for. Laying one flat on a workbench means the tool can be "laid" on it.

PICTURE THIS

If you use different chests for different things, it makes sense to put a sign on them . . . or, if you want something more visually appealing, use item frames. See how this builder has alternated double chests with single ones.

If you've made a room like this, with a high ceiling, it makes sense to put your lanterns on chains, so the light is closer to the floor.

This base mimics the curved ceilings often used by real underground spaces—curves spread the weight of the ground above, so they don't have weak points.

VILLAGE

Instead of a big house in the middle of nowhere, try building a community of smaller ones . . .

FISHING VILLAGE

When building a village, it's good to work with the landscape—like this fishing village, built right on the edge of a shore with steps leading down to the water. See how the buildings on the water have vines growing up them.

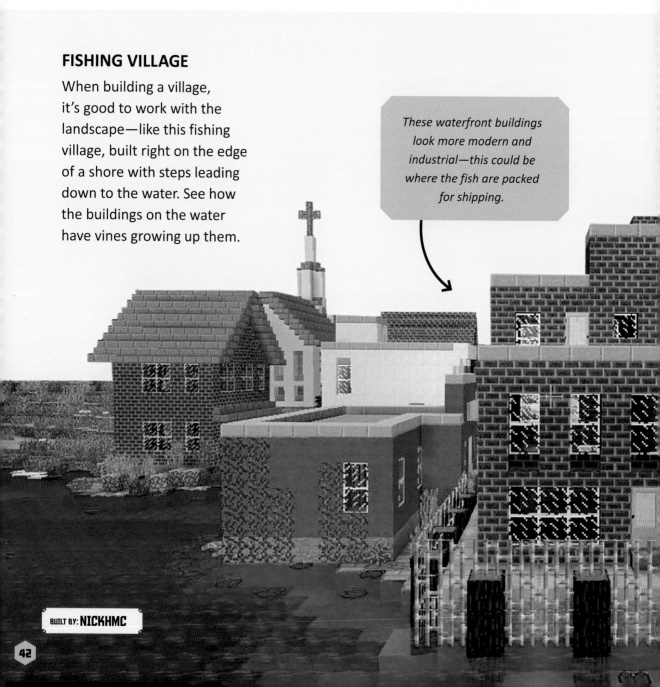

These waterfront buildings look more modern and industrial—this could be where the fish are packed for shipping.

BUILT BY: **NICKHMC**

DESERT VILLAGE

This build combines history and fantasy. The temple-like structure at the edge, next to the giant Creeper statue, was inspired by Mexican ziggurats. It's the walls that really tie this build together though, with their elegant and consistent design.

BUILT BY: **MOOFIEMOOF**

An ancient structure like this classical temple gives a sense of history to your village. Something for the tourists to see!

FLOWER SHOP

This is a great idea for a shop—there are so many different plants in *Minecraft*. Here, item frames are used to depict the seeds used to grow those plants.

BAKERY

Item frames come in handy again here, forming a picture menu over the counter. Cake can be placed like a block—and sliced! Use more item frames if you want to place other food items on the counter.

VEGETABLE PATCH

You have to place plants by water so they can grow. But why not make more of a feature of your vegetable patch than just some channels filled with water? Here they're raised, boxed in, and well lit.

VILLAGE FEATURES

Trapdoors—is there anything they can't do? Oak trapdoors are used over an ochre froglight to create a lamp post. A cauldron on a chain makes a perfect bucket for the well.

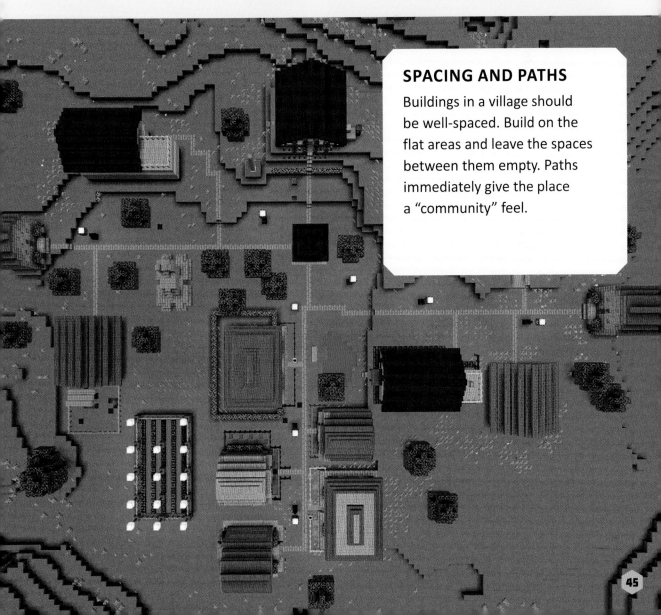

SPACING AND PATHS

Buildings in a village should be well-spaced. Build on the flat areas and leave the spaces between them empty. Paths immediately give the place a "community" feel.

WATER FEATURE

A pond is a restful community feature and doesn't need to be connected to any other water source. It can be natural-looking like this, or it can be more constructed, with paved borders. Flowers and a bench will make it more attractive.

CENTERPIECE

A statue makes a nice focal point. It doesn't have to be as huge as some of the monuments later in this book—a small and simple design can add character to a village. The copper used here has a nice weather-aged feel.

FIND YOUR PATH

Mossy stone is an essential part of any village path. This design mixes up cobblestone and stone bricks, both of which have mossy variants. You could also mix in some cracked stone bricks if you want the path to look really weathered and old.

KEEPING IT STABLE

This large stable works with the landscape instead of trying to reshape it—see how the support post on the left is higher than the one on the right. The posts also use logs rather than planks, to create the impression of whole tree trunks.

BUILT BY: SOPHIE

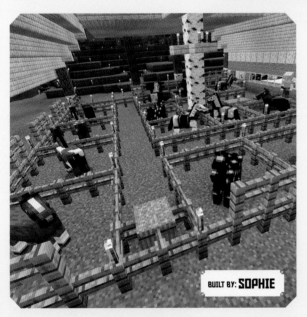

BUILT BY: SOPHIE

BUILT BY: SOPHIE

A FULL SET OF PENS

Inside the stable, we've got a network of gated pens to keep the horses in. Oak fences are a good match for the torches on the corners. If you want to name your horses, you could put signs on their pens—just remember which horse is which!

WOW YOUR COWS

Like the stable, this elegant barn uses logs for the upright posts, making it look as if the frame has been made of trunks. It's the variety of wood elements that really makes this design—the canopy over the door is actually made of unlit campfires.

Up, Up, and hWhY

Building in the sky can be used to add another dimension to your *Minecraft* world—or a touch of fantasy. Build on top of a tower of blocks, then demolish the tower to leave your creations floating free!

HOT AIR BALLOON

Take your first steps into the sky . . .

WOW, THIS BLEW UP

Balloons are not only a great introduction to sky building, they're also a great way to practice spherical builds. And then you can hang out in them and look down on your world!

BUILT BY: **TOMONMARS**

LAYERED BALLOON

This design simplifies the shape slightly by putting another layer over the main balloon, weighted with beacons that also provide light. These touches will make it look extra cool at night.

FLAME ON

Hot air balloons use a flame to heat the air and make it rise. You could mimic this with a torch, but this build uses a campfire for a more impressive effect.

A balloon isn't completely round—the top half will be spherical, but the lower half will stretch down toward the basket. The blue stripe below has a slightly different shape to the orange layer at the top.

The basket has a "woven" look, created by placing the stripped dark oak blocks so the grain runs in different directions. Experiment with how each block looks depending on what you attach it to.

GOING DOWN

Vertical stripes can be helpful in getting your balloon shape right. This one has eight purple stripes that spread outward from the top. If you build those first, you'll have a framework for the rest.

SKY PIRATES!

Avast, me hearties! Once you've worked out the shape of a balloon, you can try adding more ambitious designs like this skull and crossbones. Just make sure you don't accidentally stab your balloon with your cutlass!

RAINBOW RIDE

Balloons tend to be colorful so they stand out in the sky—which means they're a good opportunity to do a really colorful build. The strip of white with black borders across the middle of this one gives it a sense of structure.

BUILT BY: **WOLFGANG_COWBOY**

GAS AND GLASS

This is a perfect example of using materials for their appearance rather than their function. You could never make a real hot air balloon out of stained glass—but you can in *Minecraft*, and it looks amazing!

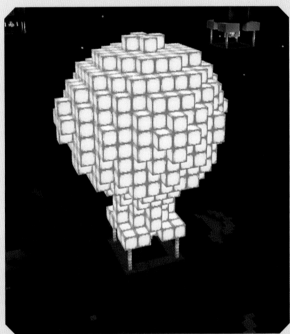

LOVE BALLOON

When working on a design like this heart, you may find it helpful to build the balloon in a single color first and get the structure right. Then you can replace blocks to create the design. Simple ones tend to work best!

LIGHTER THAN AIR

You can experiment with making balloons out of all kinds of blocks— for instance, this one is made out of sea lanterns and looks spectacular at night. What else could you try? Cactus blocks? Jack o' lanterns?

FLOATING ISLANDS

For something truly spectacular, build yourself a fantasy world in the sky!

SKY DUNGEON

This build is inspired by the Farum Azula Dungeon in the game *Elden Ring*, which has a cathedral-like dome. There's a contrast between the orderliness of the original design, with its symmetry and repeated patterns (check out the columns around the main building), and the way it's crumbling to pieces.

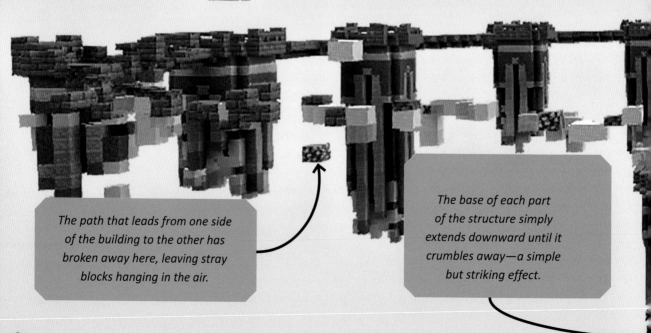

The path that leads from one side of the building to the other has broken away here, leaving stray blocks hanging in the air.

The base of each part of the structure simply extends downward until it crumbles away—a simple but striking effect.

BUILT BY: CAMBERPLAYS

WINDMILL

Winds are always stronger the higher you go, so an island in the sky is the perfect place to build a windmill. The vines on this one suggest it hasn't turned in a long time, though!

BUILT BY: LESHAGLOOM

BUILT BY: **EVERYTHINGBURRITO1**

SPACE TERMINAL

This sky build, made in the End, uses sculk for its floating island: this material glows but doesn't illuminate, which is very effective in the darkness. The heart of the tower is crying obsidian, which is luminous.

FLOATING HOUSE

If you really want to get away from it all, try taking a holiday in this cottage: it's got a beautiful garden, and we can guarantee you'll only be bothered by high-flying birds. Admittedly, it's not easy to commute to.

BUILT BY: **EVERYTHINGBURRITO1**

ISLANDS IN THE END

Another End sky build, this chain of floating islands has trails of cave vines bearing glow berries growing from them. The flowing water across the islands is a great feature, especially the water flowing off into infinity.

CHERRY BLOSSOM ISLAND

Nothing is more peaceful than a cherry blossom garden in the sky. Pink wool and dark oak give the right look for the tree; lanterns, candles, and pink glass barriers complement it perfectly.

PRIVATE BEACH

This island not only contains a little beach holiday spot, it also guarantees good weather—the glass dome will keep the rain off, while the sea lanterns mean it has its own sunshine. The coral and sea-life provide plenty for divers to discover.

CITYSCAPES

Imagine yourself as an urban planner? Or maybe you just want a really big project that you can keep on expanding. There are lots of different ways you can approach a city—you can go modern, create a world from history, or even a fantasy place . . .

BUILT BY: NICKHMC

STREET SMARTS

With cities you have to think big and small—it's the details that really make them come to life.

MODERN METROPOLIS

For a build like this you may want to start off with a completely flat world—you'll need a lot of space! An authentic-looking modern cityscape needs lots of different and interesting designs. Look at a real city skyline—the buildings weren't all built at the same time. Take inspiration from styles of building from different eras, and make use of contrasts.

The tallest buildings are likely to be the ones with a more modern style—ike this one with its swooping curve.

A mix of heights works well—real cities oftne don't have that many mega-tall skyscrapers too close together.

BUILT BY: **NICKHMC**

BUILT BY: **DRTOBIAS_FUENKE**

ANCIENT CITY

This takes a different approach to a modern city—no tall buildings and a more uniform style of architecture. Note how it uses a small color palette but creates variety by changing up the designs of walls and roofs.

BUILT BY: **NICKHMC**

BUILT BY: **NICKHMC**

SHOPS

In real cities, the ground level of an apartment or office building will often be used for shops. This creates more variety and is a good opportunity to add color, such as the awnings over these shops.

APARTMENTS

This apartment block is a great example of how real cities develop over time—the two buildings at the front are more old-fashioned, with a large extension that looks like it's been added later.

BUILT BY: **BOULI310**

FOUNTAIN

Don't crowd your cityscape with too many buildings—break it up with small parks and courtyards. This fountain is a nice, straightforward design. You could also try making a statue or some other piece of public art.

TRAIN LINE

Minecart rails aren't really the right size for an urban railway line. This design offers a simple solution: two sets of rails, side by side! This opens up fun possibilities like bridges and stations—even an underground rail network.

BUILT BY: **BOULI310**

BUILT BY: **DRTOBIAS_FUENKE**

WINDMILL

You may associate windmills with farms, but you can also add one to an old-fashioned city skyline. If you want a challenge, you can use command blocks to make a working windmill with turning blades. Good luck!

ROOFTOPS

Most tall buildings in modern cities have flat roofs, so add some realistic features: these ones use four minecart rails arranged in a circle to create an air-conditioning unit. A water tower might be another idea.

BUILT BY: **NICKHMC**

BUILT BY: **NICKHMC**

TRAFFIC LIGHTS

Real city streets have a lot of street furniture, like these traffic lights. Lamp posts, street signs, bus stops, and pedestrian crossings are other examples. Usually, the street furniture in a city will all look the same.

DESERT CITY

Here's another historical city build that uses a small color palatte. Note how it's not a flat landscape, and the design is based around one central building. This one started life as a village—just like a real city!

BUILT BY: **WOLFGANG_COWBOY**

SKYSCRAPERS

With infinite materials, the only limit on these builds is your time and patience!

HUGE HIGH-RISES

Architects on modern skyscrapers face a tricky challenge—if the design is too busy, the building will stand out too much. But without any distinctive details, the building looks dull. The same applies in *Minecraft*—you want something that's interesting to the eye but not too in-your-face.

BUILT BY: NICKHMC

OFFICE BLOCK

Putting a gray layer on every third floor of this build is a smart move—it really helps to break up the design. The floor-to-ceiling windows are the kind of thing you more commonly see on office buildings than apartments.

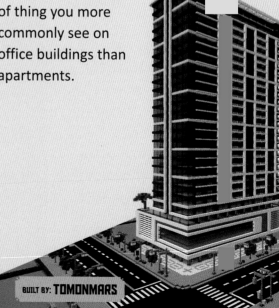

APARTMENT BLOCK

This design uses irregular chunks of light gray which protrude out from the main, dark gray block—and adds accents of red on the sides, giving some brighter color without overwhelming the appearance of the building. Unusual but subtle!

BUILT BY: TOMONMARS

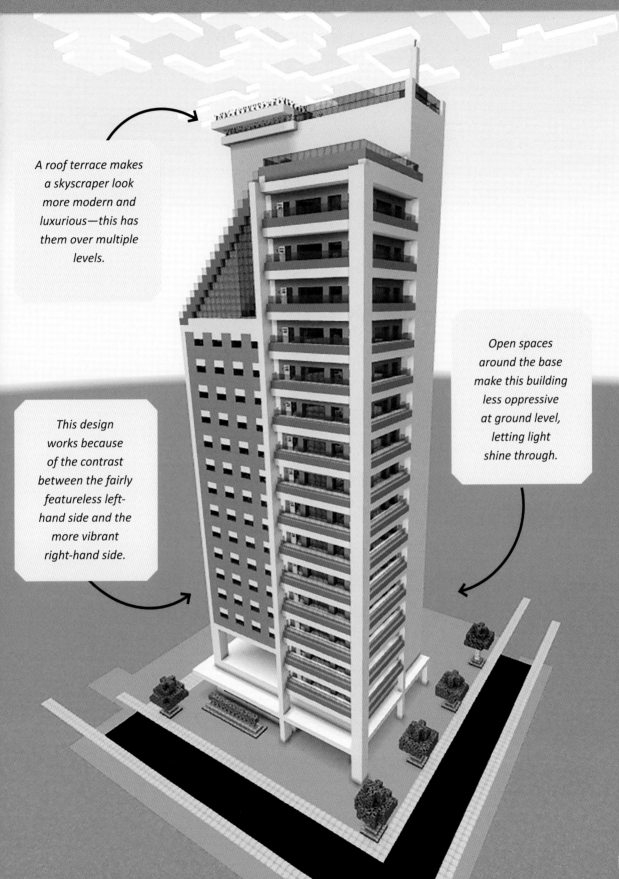

A roof terrace makes a skyscraper look more modern and luxurious—this has them over multiple levels.

Open spaces around the base make this building less oppressive at ground level, letting light shine through.

This design works because of the contrast between the fairly featureless left-hand side and the more vibrant right-hand side.

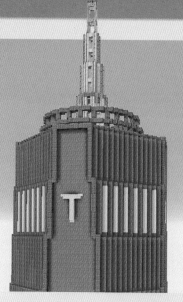

SPIRES

A spire on top of a skyscraper gives a building an elegant, mid-20th-century feel. In real life, spires are often added to make skyscrapers taller while using few materials and not adding much extra weight.

BUILDING TO A POINT

This is old-fashioned approach to skyscraper design, making the upper levels gradually smaller, has a very satisfying look. The use of quartz pillars is smart—the vertical lines really emphasise the upward-shooting structure.

BLOCKS OF COLOR

Contrasts can really help to make a city street more interesting: the old-fashioned brick building on the left here might be overwhelming if there was a whole row of them, but next to the more contemporary stone block it really pops.

SEEING DOUBLE

How do you make a skyscraper more striking? By building another one exactly the same right next to it! This design puts the two buildings at right angles on a street corner, connecting them up at the back.

BUILT BY: **TOMONMARS**

STONE-COLD CLASSIC

This functional stone design adds texture by using different types of stone block. Look at how the layers between each floor are built up—they may look like upside-down steps but they're actually layers of andesite slabs in front of stone bricks.

CITY OF GLASS

Real skyscrapers often use two-way glass, which reflects light more strongly on the outside than the inside, or some kind of tinted glass, making it easier to see out than in. This design uses cyan stained glass to mimic such effects.

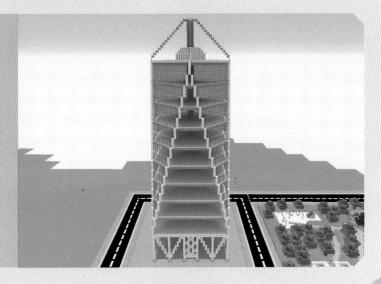

HELIPAD

This makes a skyscraper look really upmarket. If you want to put large letters on a flat surface, carpet is good because it's so thin. Alternatively, build the roof using two layers of slabs and put the design on the top layer.

OFFICE SPACE

Furnishing offices can be repetitive, so if you come up with a desk design you like, use commands to copy it. Instead of computers, each of these desks has been equipped with a book and quill in an item frame.

GREEN SPACE

A roof garden on a skyscraper offers a different kind of space. This one, in keeping with the overall design of the building, is very neatly kept, with hedges and some flowers for the bees in the hive to pollinate.

TREE-LINED

A world that's just made of metal, concrete, and glass would look bleak—trees create an immediate contrast with their different colors and organic shapes. A small loop of stone steps make an effective base.

A LIGHTER SIDE

Many modern buildings use exterior lighting to make them look more striking at night. This design incorporates a strip of end rods down one side—enough to light up the building without shining in through the windows.

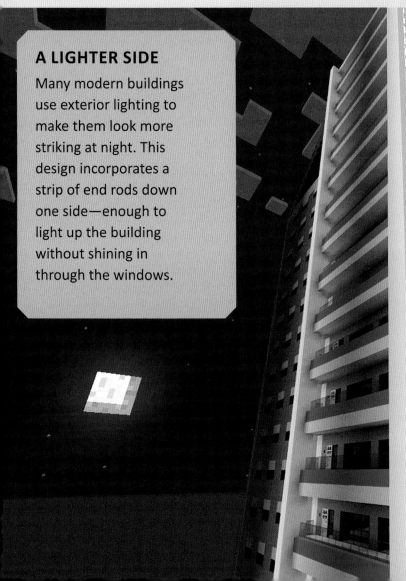

CASTLES AND PALACES

Do you want to recreate history or fly off into fantasy? Or maybe you want a luxurious royal seat or a mighty fortress? These grand old structures are well suited to *Minecraft's* pre-industrial landscape. And they tend to have fewer of those irritating curves.

CASTLES

Time to lay some medieval plans!

READY TO ROCK

Castles and *Minecraft* are an irresistible combination—the basic building material of the game, big blocks of stone, is what castles were actually made of. This means it's not too hard to make a great-looking castle, even if you're an inexperienced builder.

Here's a classic castle shape—turrets connected by walls. Plan out the distance between your turrets, and can't go too wrong.

POPULATE IT!

Villagers go very well with a castle. If you add job site blocks, your villagers will take up professions: good castle jobs include Armorer (add a blast furnace), Weaponsmith (grindstone), and Fletcher (fletching table). Then let them go about their business.

The stones with gaps between them at the top of the walls are called crenallations. Soldiers could take cover behind the stones and fire arrows through the gaps.

WALLS WITHIN WALLS

Stone bricks are the standard castle building material, but if you want to add a bit of variety to the shape, stone brick walls have lots of uses. Here, it fills the spaces in the battlements and also makes a sill for the window in this imposing turret.

STALLS WITHIN WALLS

Real castles weren't just about constant battles and sieges—they could contain whole communities with day-to-day lives. Adding a detail like this market stall also gives you a chance for some contrast with all the stone walls.

BANNERS AND TORCHES

Add a bit of color to those long stretches of stone bricks. Banners are simple and fun to make, while these impressive giant torches can be made using deepslate brick stairs and blocks of netherrack, which burns indefinitely.

HORSE STABLE

Horses were an essential part of any castle, and stables are a good thing to place against the inside of the walls. This uses a mix of mud brick walls and two types of fence to ensure the dividers between the stables aren't too thick.

BUILT BY: **SOPHIE**

BUILT BY: **SOPHIE**

BUILT BY: **SOPHIE**

AVIARY

Ideally in a castle you'd have hawks and falcons trained for hunting, but there aren't any in *Minecraft*, so parrots will have to do (they're tameable, at least). This aviary offers a number of places for birds to perch, including a feeding table.

PIG PEN

A nice touch here is that the ground isn't just bare dirt, it's dirt path that oozes under the fence and spreads out in front of the pen. Dirt path looks more like mud than the *Minecraft* block that's actually called "mud!"

BUILT BY: **LESHAGLOOM**

KNIGHT'S CASTLE

This *Elden Ring* inspired build combines many different types of stone: stone, stone bricks, chiseled stone bricks, polished andesite, diorite, deepslate, and deepslate bricks.

GOTHIC MANSION

This build uses stripped oak logs for the beams, which contrast nicely with the blackstone roofs. Gothic-style builds let you go crazy with details and additions—if you want to stick another tower on there, go for it!

BUILT BY: **LESHAGLOOM**

BUILT BY: **SQUISHYMESSESHAPPEN**

DARK FANTASY CASTLE

This build takes a classic castle shape—battlement walls with a turret on each corner—and uses a smaller version of the same shape for the inner part. The contrasting color works really well with the deepslate.

GERMANIC CASTLE

This is based on Schloss Drachenburg, a huge house built in Germany in the late 19th century—which is why it has a more modern look, with clay-based bricks rather than stone. Prismarine is used for the roof.

BUILT BY: **WOLFGANG_COWBOY**

GOTHIC CATHEDRAL

This is a perfect example of using symmetry—church-type buildings are often symmetrical, and the elaborate detailing on the front here really emphasizes this. You may find it useful to sketch a design like this before you start building!

BUILT BY: **TYTAREX**

BUILT BY: **LESHAGLOOM**

GRAND WINDOW

When making a really big window, you can fill the whole thing with glass. But in reality, a window this size would need a framework to support it, like the columns added by this builder.

FINELY DRAWN

A moat and drawbridge give a build that "castle vibe"—and they're easy to make, too. The portcullis in the doorway is also a great feature, although having it slightly raised will help you get through it!

DEFENSIVE POSITIONS

This castle is a clever variation on the classic design—the towers on either side of the entrance are pushed forward slightly. Anyone entering the front courtyard to try to break down the door will be caught between them.

ANCIENT WALLS

You can get a more weathered look on a castle by varying the texture as this build does, mixing up stone, stone bricks, and cracked stone bricks. The way the earth has crept up the walls makes it look older too.

BUILT BY: 2NIAU

BUILT BY: 2NIAU

ON THE ROCKS

This very imposing castle has been constructed on an outcrop of rock. You'd be unlikely to get a piece of land to randomly form in the right shape, so a build like this will involve a lot of work before you even start on the castle!

SNOW FORTRESS

Snow on a castle creates dramatic effects. You can build in a snowy biome, or high up in a cold biome as seen here, to get natural snow coverage. The Windswept Hills biome is a good choice.

WORLD PALACES

There's a whole world of inspiration to draw on with these monumental builds!

SPANISH-INSPIRED CASTLE

Large buildings can look more impressive as part of a landscape, and working with the landscape can make your build more interesting. See how the towers on the right-hand side of this castle are the same design but different heights—because the ground they're built on isn't level? A bit of foliage is a nice finishing touch, making the building look older.

Your main material will be often brown, pale yellow, or gray— so a more vibrant color for the roof offers a nice contrast.

A grand entrance is a great addition. The supports for this bridge and gatehouse have chunks missing, as if parts have crumbled away.

BUILT BY: CAPPENGU_YT

SHOGUN'S PALACE

This Japanese-inspired construction has distinctive curling roofs with layers—a striking style which is super fun to build. The lanterns that hang around the sides really bring it to life at night.

BUILT BY: **WOLFGANG_COWBOY**

BUILT BY: **WOLFGANG_COWBOY**

SULTAN'S PALACE

This Arabic-style design includes a domed roof that rises to a point. You may find this shape challenging to render with *Minecraft* blocks, but a little patience creates a very impressive effect.

HINDU TEMPLE

This is based on Srirangam Temple in India. When attempting a multicolor design like this, plan out your color palette by laying blocks on the ground to see how they look next to each other.

BUILT BY: **LESHAGLOOM**

WATERY WONDERS

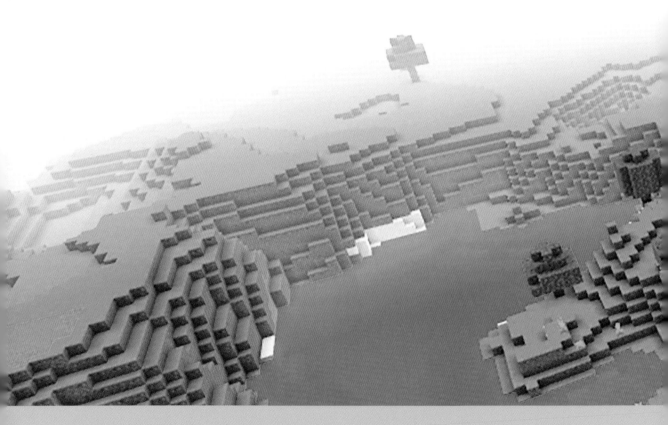

It can be easy to disregard water as something that just gets in the way of your builds. But actually it's a whole world in itself! Whether you build on top of the water or underneath it, it gives you tons of fantastic building possibilities.

SHIPS

Set sail with these majestic water-based builds!

SHIP SHAPE

Ships are easier to make in *Minecraft* than land vehicles—you don't have to worry about wheels, and they can be larger and more elegant, with interesting interiors. A ship makes a great addition to a water-based environment.

Crow's nests are a particularly fun part of shipbuilding!

The front sail, used to steer the ship, is easier to render than the others—you can just build it in a straight line.

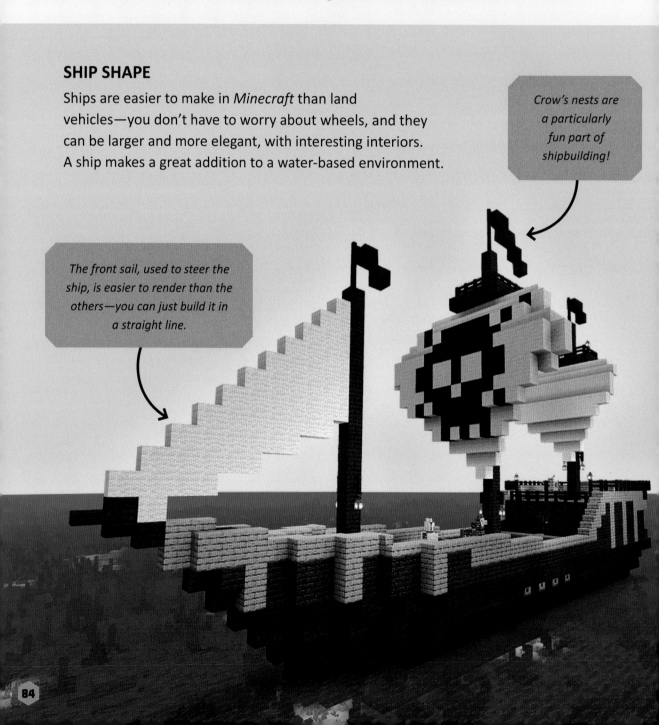

BUILT BY: **TOMONMARS**

GALLEON

The shape of a billowing sail is one of the trickiest things you could attempt in *Minecraft*, but this design pulls it off magnificently. See how the flags on the top of the masts are blowing in the same direction as the wind?

PIRATE SHIP

There are lots of neat details on this build, including the figurehead at the front of the ship and the plank for people to walk. Fences along the sides mimic the rigging that would be used to climb up to the sails.

BUILT BY: **WOLFGANG_COWBOY**

HARBOR MASTER

This shows how well ships can work as a decorative element of a world. Note how the sails are drawn up, like they would be with the ship at rest—this is easier to build!

CANNONS

No pirate ship is complete without cannons—ideally they'd have round portholes, and *Minecraft* doesn't often do round. But these dispensers have just the right look!

RED FLAGS

You could put a flag like this on top of a fence post—but here's a clever idea: put the flag at the side and let the fence connect to it. This looks more like how a flag would really be attached to a flagpole.

THE JOLLY ROGER

The classic pirate symbol isn't too hard to render in *Minecraft*—just make sure you leave enough space on your sail, and that the billow doesn't break up the design too much. This one has a good flat area in the middle.

CAPTAIN'S QUARTERS

Item frames are put to good use here, enabling a book and quill and a piece of paper to be laid on the desk. The cartography table is also a logical addition to the scene. And obviously a pirate ship has to have a parrot!

TAKE THE WHEEL!

A ship's wheel would be wooden, with handles all round it. This ingenious design uses a mangrove trapdoor and four switches to create a similar effect. It's square, but it does look wheel-ish!

BELOW DECKS

Space would've been limited on these ships, so beds would be crammed into the available room like this. The introduction of barrels as a type of chest has been very helpful to *Minecraft* shipbuilders.

LIGHTHOUSE

Avoid hitting the rocks with these striking structures!

KEEP IT LIGHT

Lighthouses were once an essential part of shipping, warning vessels not to steer too close to shore in the darkness—and there are still many in operation today. Lighthouses are usually painted white to make them easy to see, but this red-and-white striped design has become strongly associated with them. Their simple shape makes them a straightforward and satisfying project, and with a light source at the top, they'll look great at night.

This build appropriately uses sea lanterns as its light source.

Mangrove fences, doors, and trapdoors go well with the overall color scheme.

LIGHTHOUSE OF ALEXANDRIA

One of the Seven Wonders of the Ancient World, the real Lighthouse of Alexandria was made of limestone and granite—but this re-creation looks much more impressive (and lighthouse-y) in gleaming quartz.

STONE LIGHTHOUSE

Lighthouses have a long history, and there were ones in the Middle Ages which would've looked more like this. The weather vane on the roof, made from a cross of fences, is a great detail.

BUILT BY: NICKHMC

HARBOR ISLAND

Lighthouses were often built on islands in bays like this. Since the lighthouse is cut off from the land, this design includes a cottage for the lighthouse keeper—and a small jetty for boats to come in and out.

UNDERWATER BASE

Building one of these will involve some deep thinking . . .

KEEP IT TIGHT

The most frustrating part of building an underwater base is making sure it's watertight—but sponges are a great help with that, absorbing flowing sources of water as well as blocks of water. Ensure there are no gaps in your structure, place sponges until it's dry, then break the sponges (which will now be wet).

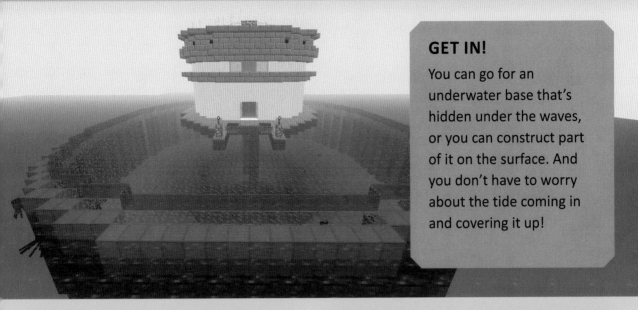

GET IN!

You can go for an underwater base that's hidden under the waves, or you can construct part of it on the surface. And you don't have to worry about the tide coming in and covering it up!

BUILT BY: SOPHIE

BUILT BY: SOPHIE

TINTED WALL

Glass works well in an underwater base, so you can see the water flowing on the other side—and you can jazz it up with a pattern of tinted glass. Sea lanterns placed at regular intervals break up the design besides providing light.

FISH TANK

You can just watch sea creatures drift past the windows of your base—or you can keep a few favorite examples in a fish tank. Making a small fish tank in *Minecraft* is difficult, so you may as well make a huge one, built into the wall.

PLUNGE POOL

In this design, the pool leads to natural underwater caves: you'll need to add water sources on the "dry" side to make sure the pool is level, since the water will flow downward.

ARMOR DISPLAY

Armor stands work nicely as decoration in a grand location like this. They can be placed at different angles and in different poses, so you can be creative with how you arrange them.

WATER WINDOW

This window sets the level of the pool, and the other side is underwater, providing views on the subaquatic world beyond. If you've built into a dark area like a cave, a few sea lanterns may improve the view.

TERRACOTTA RUG

An aqua color scheme of blue and turquoise works well for an undersea location. This rug is created from blocks of glazed terracotta set into the floor. Positioning them correctly to make a pattern can take time, though.

DEEP READING

Most of this base is subtly lit by sea lanterns in the ceilings, walls and floors—but this library area switches it up by using a froglight. Just make sure those books don't get damp . . .

SEAFOOD

This kitchen area includes some clever details—the cabinets are barrels, so you can actually store things in them! The block above the furnace is actually a loom. Prismarine brick chairs match the aqua color scheme used elsewhere.

NATURAL ARCHITECTURE

Make your world a little wilder with these natural (and not-so-natural) structures! These designs demand a more organic approach than normal *Minecraft* builds, so practice your cylinders and domes—and join us as we head into the woods . . .

TREE HOUSE

"Wood" you like to live in one of these?

FIRST, BUILD YOUR TREE

You can build on top of the natural features of your world or grow trees and build onto them (spruce and jungle saplings can be planted in a clump of four to grow into a giant variety).

But if you want a bigger "natural" structure, like the one on the opposite page, so you can build inside it—then you'll need to build it yourself.

TOADSTOOL HOUSE

This mutant toadstool has big *Alice In Wonderland* vibes. Wool has been used for the cap and quartz has been used for the stalk—but an alternative would be to use colored concrete and mushroom stem.

VIEWING PLATFORM

Your tree house can be entirely concealed inside the tree—or you can have parts of it emerging from the leaves, like this room with floor-to-ceiling windows and an infinite waterfall. It's perfectly safe!

Making natural-looking shapes can be tricky—this giant tree doesn't have one single peak, it has a few.

We suggest you build in a clear, open space—you don't want other trees getting in the way.

TALL ORDER

This is a nice, simple tree design—a straight, regular cylinder which can be built in a fairly small space, with the living area at the top. With the connecting bridges, you could make a whole complex of tree houses.

BUILT BY: **JAMES**

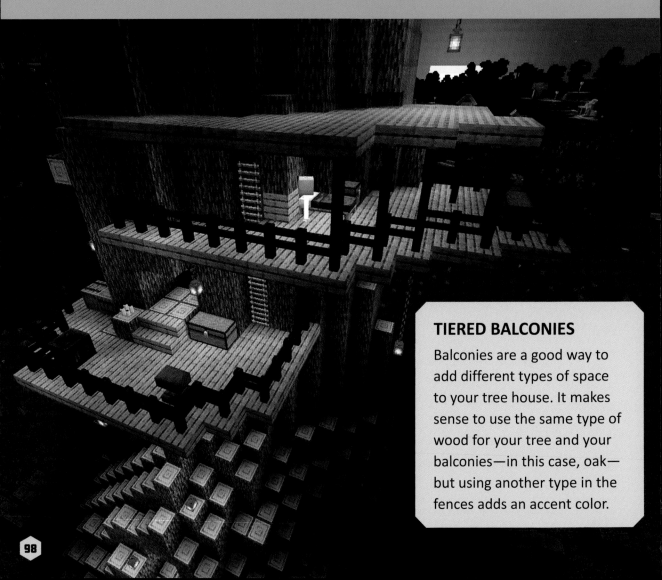

TIERED BALCONIES

Balconies are a good way to add different types of space to your tree house. It makes sense to use the same type of wood for your tree and your balconies—in this case, oak—but using another type in the fences adds an accent color.

TREE CLIMBING

The spiral staircase inside the tree is narrow. This design incorporates a bannister without making the stairs too wide by attaching a fence post to a block beneath each step and then placing two more posts on top.

BRANCH OUT

Remember, leaves need to be no more than six blocks away from a log block, otherwise they die and disappear. You may not be able to see the branches inside this treetop, but they're there! Make sure you add them to yours.

NETHER PORTAL

Adding to the general weirdness of this giant tree, it's got a knot partway up its trunk with a nether portal inside. This has simply been built vertically and then the logs laid over it—notice how the grain on all the wood runs upward.

GARDENS AND PARKS

Everyone needs a little green space—even if it's on a computer screen.

LAWN AND ORDER

Gardens and parks are about putting natural elements into a human-made design—in real life and in *Minecraft*. Gardens look good in all kinds of builds, from mansions and cabins to villages and cities.

Here's a really simple but effective layout—the garden is divided into quarters, each with a different function and theme.

WELL DONE

Water-related features work nicely in a garden or park, and this well works beautifully—the overgrown aspects make it look disused. If you have a sizable pond in your park, you could try placing a fountain in it.

BUILT BY: **SOPHIE**

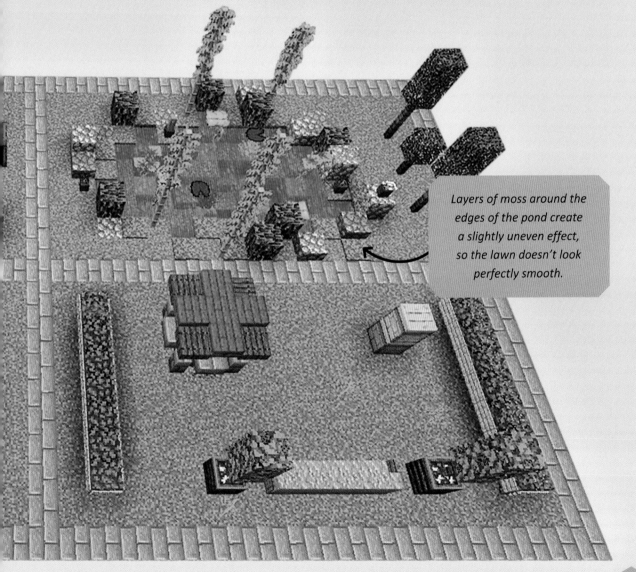

Layers of moss around the edges of the pond create a slightly uneven effect, so the lawn doesn't look perfectly smooth.

GREENHOUSE

A greenhouse makes a great addition to a house with a large garden. A mix of plants that grow upward and downward makes it look much denser with vegetation—the weeping vines are an especially striking element.

ROOF GARDEN

A roof garden will usually be well-looked-after and organiszd, so this one has small, constructed trees that don't dominate the space, as well as neat rows of plants. The beehive in the tree is a nice touch.

SWIMMING POOL

Glazed terracotta blocks are perfect for builds like this, and the blue-and-yellow design has big sunshine vibes. Don't overuse it, or the design will be too busy—the edge of the pool area, the tiled wall, and the base of the pool itself is enough.

PLANT DISPLAY

Some of the plants in a real garden may be kept in pots—and in *Minecraft* a pot will prevent a sapling growing into a full tree. This table arranges them neatly under a canopy of leaves, arranged on a framework made of fences.

GAME BOARD

A nice, slow-paced board game is a perfect match for this setting. It's hard to find something that makes a good chess board, but you can experiment with different objects in an item frame—this one uses a black banner.

BEE ONE WITH NATURE

This seating area incorporates a small well and beehives. The trees here have been planted in composters, which nicely echo the stripes on the bees. A hedgerow at the side is kept tidy with a small "fence"—actually just a row of blank signs.

STATUES AND MONUMENTS

These builds let you get really creative—and you can place them anywhere you like. They can be all on their own in the middle of nowhere or right in the heart of a city. Give your visitors some awesome sights to discover!

STATUES

Here's a chance to show off your artistic side . . .

BIGGER IS BETTER

Trying to make something look like a person or an animal in *Minecraft* is tricky when you're working with a small number of blocks. If you work on a larger scale, you can create more detailed shapes. So while a statue can be a large and challenging project, it's worth going big.

STONE HEAD

Something like this is a good first project for a statue builder—it's not too large, and the basic shape is straightforward. It's also symmetrical, so if you get one side right, you can definitely get the other side right!

COLOSSUS OF RHODES

The original of this was another of the Seven Wonders of the Ancient World—this ambitious reworking places it across a bay so boats pass between its legs. Dark prismarine makes the torch.

With statues, you can work in just one color, which makes things simpler—the block of emerald for the eye is a great detail.

This cat statue has one paw reaching forward, which really helps bring it to life.

MONUMENTS

Make your mark on the world with some epic builds!

THINK BIG

Whether you're recreating a real-life monument or inventing one of your own, this is one of the most fun types of building. It doesn't necessarily have to have a function—it just has to look spectacular! This kind of structure is usually symmetrical.

GREAT SPHINX OF GIZA

This ancient Egyptian Sphinx is simpler to build than an upright statue, since it lies flat on the ground. The real one is made of limestone, but this uses smooth sandstone: it also adds back some of the colors that have worn away over the centuries.

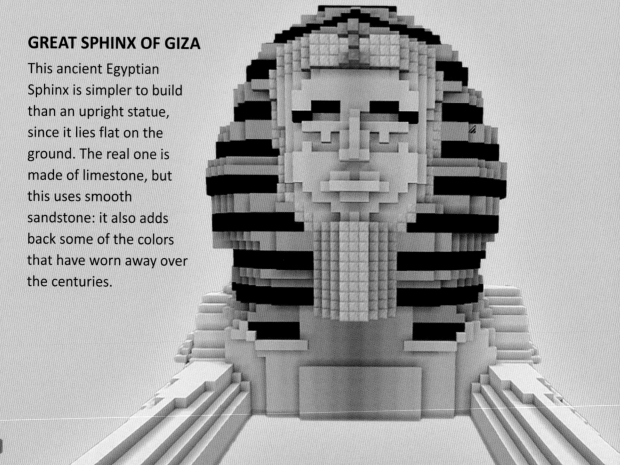

MEDIEVAL DOME

This original creation is an expert example of spherical building. The interior features walkways lined with gardens as well as an inner chamber. The main materials are brick and granite for the supports, and spruce planks for the domes.

BUILT BY: 2NIAU

PARTHENON

The Parthenon temple in Athens is partly ruined now, but this model restores it to its ancient glory. The carvings of classical figures on the roof have been represented here by light-colored armor stands.

MAYAN TEMPLE

Important Mayan buildings were raised high off the ground, and temples makes fun *Minecraft* projects, with their large, impressive bases. This design removes a few stones from the base and adds overgrown vegetation to age it.

BUILT BY: PPLLAYZ

REDSTONE BASICS

Mastering redstone is an essential part of mastering *Minecraft*. Redstone blocks enable you to add power to objects in your world, as well as creating electrical circuits that connect your redstone blocks to switches and pistons. Redstone makes your worlds more interactive and can create automated processes with things like farming.

REDSTONE

It's time to get things moving with this game-changing block!

MEET THE FAMILY

One of the most exciting items in *Minecraft* is redstone. Its potential is massive, and although redstone is itself a block, there are plenty of other items that fall into the redstone family, such as pistons, doors, pressure plates, and more.

HERE WE GO . . .

In this section, we will show some of the most basic concepts so that you can start adding your own redstone contraptions to your builds. Almost anything built in Creative with redstone could also be achieved in Survival, but it can be pushed even further in Creative Mode with code blocks and commands.

PRACTICE MAKES PERFECT

Try to experiment with ideas yourself in Creative Mode. Perhaps set up a practice world to try different things inspired by what you see here. There is a massive amount of amazing material about redstone online. There are even instructions on how to build working computers INSIDE the game!

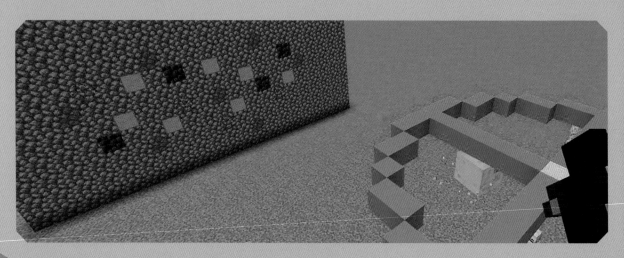

Block of Redstone

Redstone torch

Redstone dust

Redstone Repeater

Redstone Comparator

Redstone Lever

WHO? WHAT? WHERE?

Before you can use redstone, you need to know the basic tools. In the picture above, you can see a block of redstone and a redstone torch. They act as power sources. There is also redstone dust, which can be used like a power cable between components. There is a redstone repeater and a redstone comparator—both of which affect a redstone dust signal—and a lever, which is a type of component that can turn power sources on or off.

REDSTONE POWER

Redstone power sources will output a signal strength of 15. Here, we've used a redstone lamp to show that if a power source is more than 15 blocks away, the lamp doesn't receive power. A repeater can be used to output a fresh value of 15, meaning you can then extend your circuits beyond 15 blocks.

SPREADING THE POWER

Redstone torches won't power the block they are placed on, but they will power the blocks above and next to them. A block powered by a redstone torch can also give out power.

The redstone on the left won't light either lamp. But the redstone on the right is able to power the lamps surrounding it, which are in turn powering the lamps directly next to them. There is also power going to the lamp via the redstone dust.

REDSTONE BLOCK

A redstone block will power the blocks it directly interacts with and can also send power through redstone dust.

FLIP THE SWITCH

A lever can be used to power a block, which can directly power a redstone component such as a lamp and is extremely useful as a basic light switch.

REDSTONE DUST

Redstone dust can only send power to certain blocks. Here, we can see that it won't power items above it or next to it on the ground, but will send power directly into a block or a block *in* the ground next to it. This is because the redstone dust is powering the block below, which is connected to the lamp. A repeater or comparator can draw a signal from it and then be used to power a block.

Running redstone dust from a switch to a lamp can be used to power or depower your redstone dust, essentially acting as an on or off switch.

OFF   ON

COMPARATORS

A comparator is a unique device that can measure the strength of more than one signal and then give a different output based on its settings.

Where a repeater will give out a signal strength of 15, a comparator will not. A comparator will give out a signal strength equal to what it receives. On the left side, the redstone dust length from the power source to the comparator is 9, meaning it's receiving a signal strength of 6 (15 - x = y). This means it's giving out a signal strength of 6, which is enough power to reach the lamp.

However, the lamp in the middle is not powered. This is because the redstone line from the power source to the comparator is 5, meaning the signal strength output is 5, and therefore the power cannot reach the lamp.

You can see the repeater on the right, drawing power from the comparator's weak signal, is still able to output a full 15 signal strength.

SUBTRACT MODE

Comparators have two modes: subtract mode and normal mode. In subtract mode, where the light on the front is switched on, the comparator will give out a signal strength based on subtracting the signal values running in from the rear and the side. In this case it receives 8 from the source and 6 from the side, (8 - 6 = 2), so it will give out a signal strength of 2.

You can see that the longer redstone line being activated causes the second lamp to lose power, as it's now giving a weaker output signal.

COMPLEX CIRCUITRY

Don't worry if this seems complicated at first. With redstone, it's pretty easy to experiment until you get it right.

Let's take a look at some of the other things that redstone can do, and you'll start to see how all of this information can be put to use . . .

QUICK PULSE

Buttons can also be used to power blocks. Here we show that a button placed on a block adjacent to a piston can provide power. A button can also be placed directly onto the piston itself for power. The power is only momentary though, so switches are best for sending quick pulses through circuits.

PRESSURE PLATES

Similarly, pressure plates can also be used in this way. Wooden pressure plates can be triggered by dropping items directly on top of them.

OBSERVERS

An observer will detect any changes to the blocks in front of it and output a redstone pulse. This powers whatever is placed behind it.

HIT THE MARK

A target block will also give a redstone output if hit by an arrow.
In fact, the closer to bullseye, the stronger the signal it outputs.
Hitting the middle means more power will be supplied to whatever
you've connected the target block to.

TRIPWIRE

A tripwire will also send out a redstone pulse, if tripped or
broken by a player (unless they use shears).

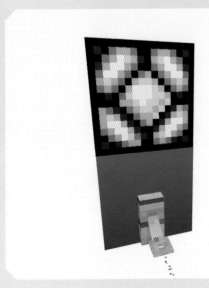

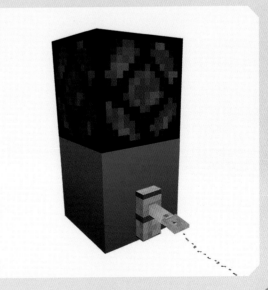

DROP THAT PIG!

Droppers and dispensers are great redstone components with all sorts of uses. Whether it's for fun surprises, ruthless traps, or as part of equipping for a mini game, a dropper will simply drop an item. Here, when we placed a pig egg inside and used a lever to activate it, it dropped an egg for us. A dispenser, however, will give us a pig. Dispensers can also fire projectiles, such as arrows or fireworks. They make great traps when combined with pressure plates or tripwires.

DAYLIGHT DETECTOR

A daylight detector can be used to identify the time of day and give out a redstone signal depending on its settings. Here, it is set to night mode, so will only give out power at night. This can be great for setting time limits in any team games you build.

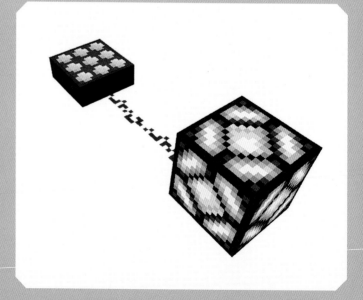

PRANK PREP

Comparators can also be used to draw redstone output from some items. A comparator can receive power from a chest, but the signal output will be determined by how many items are in the chest. The chest on the left is empty, so doesn't give an output, but the chest on the right has items in it.

POWER OF THE PAGES

With a lectern, the power output is determined by a book and the book's number of pages. A 15-page book can give out 15 different levels of signal, depending on the page it is turned to. Not bad if you're looking to build a jump scare for your friends!

REMOTE ACCESS

While levers and buttons can be used to open doors and trapdoors, redstone dust can be used to make that happen remotely. Remember, redstone doesn't have to be one level—you can build up and down with redstone, as shown with our door.

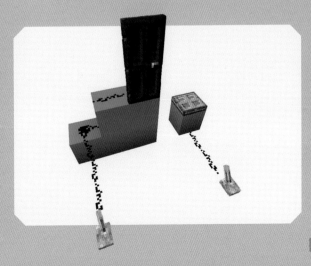

RIDE THE RAILS

It's no surprise that minecarts can have redstone rails in *Minecraft*. These rails can be used to help your minecarts perform different functions. A powered rail will push your minecart along but only for a few blocks, so you will need multiple power sources along a rail track if you want to go any great distance.

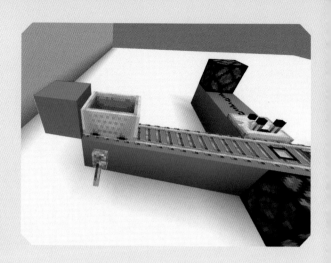

DETECTOR RAIL

A detector rail is exactly what it sounds like. It detects when a minecart passes over and sends out a pulse. You can see the lamp is illuminated when the cart is on the rail.

TRAVEL CHEST

A comparator can be used to draw power from minecarts with chests, proportional to how many items are in the chests.

ENDING WITH A BANG!

An activator rail is also quite self-explanatory—carts passing over will receive a pulse—so a minecart carrying dynamite will be triggered as it passes over the activator rail.

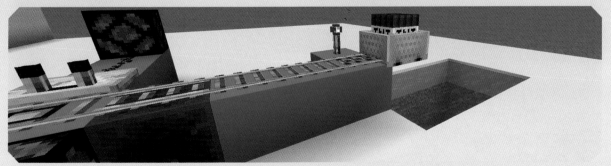

ULTIMATE BUILDING CHALLENGES

Are you up for doing something a bit more unusual? A build that goes beyond the obvious? Try one of our building challenges—we'll give you some inspiration, but the more original and inventive you can be, the better your build will be!

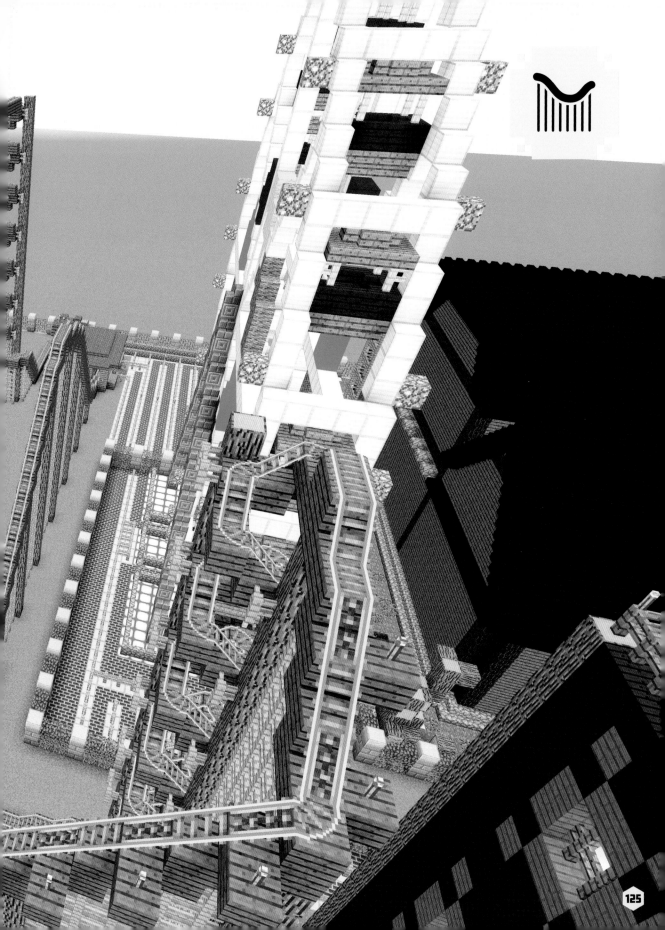

CHALLENGE 1:
NETHER PORTAL

A Nether Portal can look like anything. So why not make it look really cool?

GOING DARK

A Nether Portal naturally suggests dark vibes—for instance, this one uses a mix of blackstone and deepslate—and it's also a good place to break out those floating island skills, in this case over a pit of lava. Looks toasty warm!

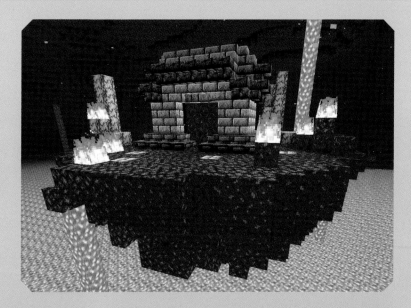

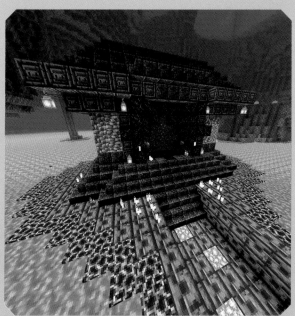

BUILT BY: **EVERYTHINGBURRITO1**

EXPANDED PORTAL

Crying obsidian is a good match for the colors of the portal, and this design surrounds the portal with the stuff to give it a more three-dimensional appearance. Candles give the whole thing a solemn, ceremonial look.

MYSTERIOUS PORTAL

This design is perfect for a secluded spot in the forest, with its overgrown vines. Again, purple details have been used to echo the purple of the portal—tinted glass on the floor and amethysts on the corners, which look great against the greenery.

CHALLENGE 2:
THEME PARK

Dream up some wild rides for this colorful challenge! It's cheaper than going to a real one . . .

ROLLER COASTER

This is one of the most enjoyable things to make in *Minecraft*, due to the fact that working rails and minecarts mean you can actually ride it after it's built. But what else could you add? Some spooky tunnels filled with mobs, maybe?

FERRIS WHEEL

Wheel out your circular building skills! The bigger you make your Ferris wheel, the more smoothly circular it can be. If you want a really advanced project, it's possible to use mods to make a Ferris wheel that *turns* . . .

CHALLENGE 3:
CUTE ART

Go 2D for these too-cute designs!

LOOK HERE

Creating flat art in *Minecraft* allows you to work in a different style. It's basically pixel art and is well suited to bold, cartoony images. Colored concrete is the best material for this, though you can experiment with adding others. You can build flat on the ground, as part of a wall, or have it free-standing.

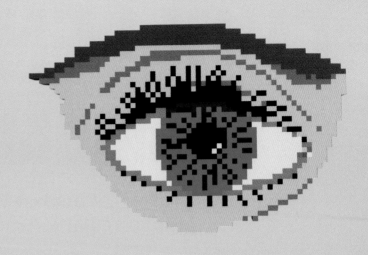

RAINBOW UNICORN

Cute art is a good chance to go really colorful in a way you probably wouldn't when making buildings. Note how the rainbow strands of the unicorn's hair aren't all the same width, because real hair doesn't fall in a uniform way—especially when it sweeps and curves like this.

OCTOPUS

A little shading can give shape to a design. This uses magenta as its main color, with pink suggesting light shining from the top right, while purple creates shade on the opposite side. Cyan, as used on the dolphin to the left, also works well with the two blue blocks as light and shade.

CHALLENGE 4:
BRIDGES

Don't get cross—get across! Span spaces with spectacular structures.

COVERED BRIDGE

Bridges don't have to be open—you can add more of a structure. This design, with its canopy and lanterns, is like one you might find in a Chinese-style garden. The mix of mossy stone walls and wood fences gives an unusual, eye-catching effect.

BUILT BY: **EVERYTHINGBURRITO1**

TREETOP BRIDGE

This bridge connects one treetop hut to another, stepping up to account for the different heights. Sticking to wood means the bridge and huts match the environment. You could create a whole network of these.

CAVERN BRIDGE

This bridge blends nicely with its surroundings, using stone and underhanging foliage. Raising the brick wall up on a series of posts gives a different effect to the usual brick wall. Blocks of amethyst in the supports add a little something extra.

MINECRAFT CREATIVE QUIZ

TEST YOUR CREATIVE KNOWLEDGE

So, think you know Creative Mode? Let's test your knowledge. You can always check back through the book if you're stuck . . .

01 What are the three main advantages of Creative Mode?

02 How many main categories of biome are there?

03 What's the main dimension of *Minecraft* called?

04 What are the other two dimensions called?

05 Which mode prevents mobs from spawning?

06 What three letters represent your coordinates when using the fill command?

07 When writing coordinates, what symbol can you can use to refer to your own position?

08 Name five types of wood found in *Minecraft*.

09 Which two types of stone block can be mossy?

10 What type of mod can be used to alter the light in a *Minecraft* world?

11 How can you make a record player?

12 Why do mob skulls make good ornaments?

13 Which food item in *Minecraft* can be sliced?

14 How can you make an air-conditioning unit?

15 Which game inspired the Sky Dungeon featured in the Floating Islands section?

16 What type of block gives professions to villagers?

17 What two types of bird can currently be found in *Minecraft*?

18 What block absorbs water?

19 What type of block has the most decorative patterns on its surfaces?

20 How close do leaves need to be to a log block?

21 How can you prevent a sapling growing?

22 What's the signal strength of a redstone power source?

23 Where must a block be placed to get power from a redstone torch?

24 What are the two modes of a redstone comparator?

25 What's the difference between a dropper and a dispenser?

26 What determines the power of a lectern when hooked up to a redstone circuit?

27 What can be placed in a minecart to enable a comparator to draw power from it?

28 What two colors can be used to add shading to a piece of cute art made with magenta concrete?

QUIZ ANSWERS

1 You can't die, you have unlimited materials, and you can fly.

2 Seven.

3 The Overworld.

4 The Nether and the End.

5 Peaceful Mode.

6 X, Y, and Z.

7 The tilde symbol (~).

8 Any five from: oak, spruce, birch, jungle, acacia, dark oak, crimson, warped, or mangrove.

9 Cobblestone and stone bricks.

10 Shaders.

11 Place a music disc into an item frame.

12 They can be placed at diagonal angles.

13 Cake.

14   Place four minecart rails in a circle.

15   *Elden Ring.*

16   Job site blocks.

17   Parrots and chickens.

18   Sponge.

19   Glazed terracotta.

20   Six blocks.

21   Plant it in a pot.

22   15.

23   Above or next to it.

24   Subtract mode and normal mode.

25   A dropper will simply drop an egg that's been placed inside it, whereas a dispenser will dispense the creature.

26   The number of pages in the book that's placed on the lectern.

27   A chest.

28   Pink and purple.

DREAM BUILD CHECKLIST

Your favorite building in
your home town.. ⬡

A ten-story skyscraper with
a swimming pool on top .... ⬡

A hot air balloon with a view of
the mountains.. ⬡

A luxury beachside hotel .... ⬡

A castle or palace—on a floating island............ ⬡

An underwater base with its own
Nether Portal .... ▢

A mega-sized treehouse .... ▢

A cat cafe .... ▢

A theater—or a sports stadium .... ▢

A statue of a friend, family member,
or pet .... ▢

A statue of yourself, which you
can live inside .... ▢

A roller coaster that peaks at more than
twenty blocks high .... ▢

ACKNOWLEDGMENTS

We would like to thank the builders below, who created the wonderful builds in The Ultimate Guide to *Minecraft* Creative Mode.

Ben Westwood	CamberPlays
Sophie Pierce	Leshagloom
James Anderson	DrTobias_Fuenke
NickHmc	Bouli310
Tomonmars	SquishyMessesHappen
Gabriel Robson Spooner	TytaRex
Everythingburrito1	2niau
Moofiemoof	CapPengu_YT
Wolfgang_cowboy	PPLLAYZ